Lists

Easy Word Essentials
Volume 3

M.L. HUMPHREY

TITLES BY M.L. HUMPHREY

EASY WORD ESSENTIALS
Text Formatting
Page Formatting
Lists
Tables
Track Changes

WORD ESSENTIALS
Word for Beginners
Intermediate Word

MAIL MERGE ESSENTIALS
Mail Merge for Beginners

CONTENTS

INTRODUCTION

In *Word for Beginners* I covered the basics of working in Word and in *Intermediate Word* I covered more intermediate-level topics. But I realized that some users will just want to know about a specific topic and not buy a guide that covers a variety of other topics that aren't of interest to them.

So this series of guides is meant to address that need. Each guide in the series covers one specific topic such as formatting, tables, or track changes.

I'm going to assume in these guides that you have a basic understanding of how to navigate Word, although each guide does include an Appendix with a brief discussion of basic terminology to make sure that we're on the same page.

The guides are written using Word 2013, which should be similar enough for most users of Word to follow, but anyone using a version of Word prior to Word 2007 probably won't be able to use them effectively.

Also, keep in mind that the content in these guides is drawn from *Word for Beginners* and *Intermediate Word*, so if you think you'll end up buying all of these guides you're probably better off just buying *Word for Beginners* and *Intermediate Word* instead.

Having said all of that, let's talk bulleted and numbered lists.

BULLETED LISTS

A bulleted list is just what it sounds like, a list of items where each line starts with a bullet mark on the left-hand side. The most common bullet choice is probably a small dark black circle that's filled in, but Word has a few options you can choose from:

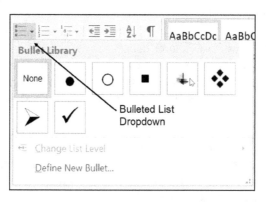

To create a bulleted list, go to the Paragraph section of the Home tab and click on the bulleted list dropdown menu to select the type of bullet you want to use in your list.

If you know that what you're about to type is going to be a bulleted list, you can click on the bulleted list option before you start typing. Word will insert the bullet you've chosen and move the cursor to where your text will start.

If you've already typed the first row of text that you want bulleted, you can click on the bulleted list option you want while in that row of text and it will convert it to the first entry of a bulleted list.

Hitting enter at the end of the line in a bulleted list, will start a new line with a bullet.

Or, last but not least, if all of your text has already been entered you can select all of the lines that you want to be part of the bulleted list and then choose the bulleted list option and it should convert your text to a bulleted list with one bullet per paragraph or individual line.

If you have a line that's bulleted and you don't want it to be, you can go to the beginning of the text on that line and backspace. Once will remove the bullet. Twice will move the text to the beginning of the line. Or, you can select the line and choose None from the bulleted list dropdown menu.

(You can also use the Format Painter to apply bullets to a list of entries or to remove them depending on the formatting of your source data.)

Another way to create a bulleted list is to select your text and then right-click to bring up the mini formatting menu. The bulleted list dropdown is one of the available options.

With bulleted lists, Word automatically indents your text. If you don't want that, you can use the Decrease Indent option (on the top row of the Paragraph section of the Home tab) to move the text back to the left-hand side of the page but keep the bullets.

NUMBERED LISTS

You can also create a "numbered" list that uses letters or numbers for each entry in your list instead of bullets.

One easy way to create a numbered list in more recent versions of Word is to simply type the first number you want to use, the separator mark you want, and then a space. Word will automatically indent that entry and turn it into the first entry in a numbered list. So, for example, I might type the number 1 followed by a period and then a space. Word will indent that 1. and make it the first entry in my list. This works with all of the options on the dropdown menu we're about to look at. (This is part of the Autocorrect settings, so a little thunderbolt will appear next to the number when this first happens. If you don't want that to happen, you can click on the arrow next to the thunderbolt and have Word reverse the change by telling it to Undo Automatic Numbering.)

When you hit enter after typing in the text for your first line, Word will continue the numbering you started.

The other option, especially if you already have your list and just need to convert it to a numbered list, is to select the lines you want to number, go to the Home tab and in the Paragraph section click on the arrow next to the

Numbering option and choose the numbered list option you want from there.

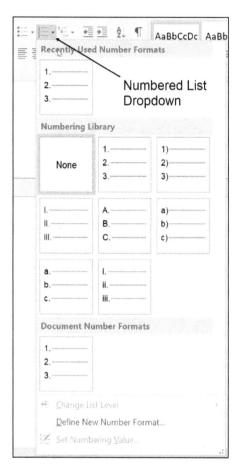

As you can see, you have the option to choose between lists that use 1, 2, 3 or i, ii, iii or A, B, C or a, b, c, or I, II, III and then between using a period after the "number" or a paren. For a basic list, this should be all you really need.

When you right-click on your list you'll also see that the mini formatting menu is available and that one of the options is the numbering option. So instead of going to the Home tab, you could just right-click and choose from there to create your numbered list.

You can also create two-level or three-level lists by using the tab key to indent your numbering or the shift and tab keys together to decrease the indent on your numbering. This gives you, for example, a first level that is 1, 2, 3 with the option of a second level under that that's a, b, c. To do this, go to each line you want to be second-level (or third-level) and use the tab key to indent that line. This will change the numbering of the line at the same time it moves it inward.

If you need very fine control over a multi-level list or you need a list that works throughout your document and has lots of breaks in it, you'll probably want to use the Multilevel List option instead.

If you had a numbered list earlier in your document and want that numbering to continue in the location where you are now, you can do that. Or, if Word continued the numbering and you wanted it to start over at 1, you can do that, too. In either case, you're going to right-click on the number you want to change. You'll then either choose Continue Numbering (to continue from a prior section) or Set Numbering Value (to change the value you start with back to 1 or A or whatever you're using).

MULTILEVEL LISTS

I truly hate working with multilevel lists. At their most basic they are wonderful and a God-send. But when you're working for a company that requires its own custom version of a multilevel list with non-standard levels and bizarre indents, they're a nightmare to set up and a nightmare to get others to use properly. Which means hours wasted trying to fix them.

Multilevel lists are essentially a more complex version of numbered lists that use various letters and numbering to provide a standard outline format. Like this:

I. **Level One Item**

    A. *Level Two Item*

        1. Level Three Item

            a) **Level Four Item**

Word provides a number of pre-formatted choices you can use to create one of these lists.

The problem is, they never seem to be what you want them to be. Like the one I used above. The first three levels are fine, but then it goes for the lower-case a with a paren instead of a lower-case a with a period which is what I'd expect.

That might seem like a silly distinction to make. I mean, really, who cares if you use a paren instead of a period? Well, let me tell you…Lots of managers do. I've worked for companies that have spent hundreds of thousands of dollars on petty little differences like this. (And I will also admit that my mild obsessive compulsive tendencies are also annoyed by it.)

So there's that. The templates that Word oh so helpfully provides aren't ones you can use in most situations.

The other issue I have with them is that they change formatting in other parts of your document when you're not looking. When I started to write this section, I made the mistake of creating that example of a multilevel list that I used above in this document. Word changed all of my chapter headers. It converted all of them over to the formatting for level one items on that list because they use the Heading 1 style. Suddenly every single chapter heading in this document was numbered. All because I tried to use a pre-built multilevel list in one section of my document.

Now, I'm not saying don't use multi-level lists. I'm just saying be very careful if you do choose to use them. Ideally, do not use any other numbering or bulleting or headers in a document that uses them. They have to provide the entire structure of your document or you'll end up spending hours fixing your document.

So.

If you do need to use a multilevel list, how do you do it?

Let me tell you a way to avoid using them altogether first. Then we'll dive into using the actual multilevel list option.

If you insert a numbered list into Word (using the Numbering option in the Paragraph tab that was discussed above), you can turn that list into a list with multiple levels by using the tab key or the increase indent option.

To do this, start your first line with a capital I followed by a period and a space. Word will automatically convert that to the first entry in a numbered list. Type a value for that first entry. It doesn't have to be your final text, but you do need text on this line. (Otherwise if you hit enter it will disappear.)

Now, hit enter. Word will automatically continue the numbered list and start the next row with the number two (II) followed by a period and space. To create a secondary level for your multilevel list, hit Tab or use the Increase Indent option in the Paragraph section of the Home tab.

Word will turn that two (II) into a lower-case a. When you type text into that line and hit enter, it will number the next row with a lower-case b. (You can use Shift + Tab or Decrease Indent from the Paragraph section of the Home tab to move back one level to a II.)

Or you can create a third level for your list that will be numbered with lower-case roman numerals (i, ii, iii, etc.) by using tab or increasing the indent.

If at any point using the tab keys or the indent options doesn't change the list level, type some text on that line and then go to the beginning of the text and try again. Sometimes, for whatever reason, Word will only change the list level if there's already text entered on that line and then only if you position your cursor at the start of where the text is.

If you do what I just described, you can get a multilevel list that looks like this and is pretty easy to work with:

I. Heading One

    a. Heading Two

        i. Heading Three

           1. Heading Four

Problem is, that's not standard format. Usually you'd expect to see the upper-case Roman numeral (I) followed by an upper case letter A and then lower-case versions of both. That lower-case a in the second level is incorrect.

You can try to force the list into standard format by going to each level of the list and choosing the appropriate letter/number and format for that level, but then the spacing between the number and the text becomes inconsistent and using the indent options stops working. You can fix these things, but they're not stable and will sometimes revert to their old formatting unexpectedly. You'll change an indent on page ten and the indent on page two will go back to its original form with no warning or notice. The only way you'll know is by looking back through your document.

The other option you have, of course, is the multilevel list option.

To create a multilevel list, type in the text you want for your first entry, click on that line of text, and choose an option from the multilevel list options.

Unlike with the Numbering option, you can't just hit enter and have the next line automatically be included in the list. When you hit enter, you'll be back to plain text. To change that next line to part of the list, once again select the list from the multilevel list dropdown. If you want this line to be indented one level, you can use the tab key or the indent option once you've chosen the list from the menu.

The nice thing about each line not being automatically included in the list is that this lets you have sections of text underneath each entry in your list. Like this:

> I. Heading One
>
> So this is where you'd discuss the key parts covered by this section in your document.
>
> > a. Heading Two
> >
> > And then you'd add more text that talks about the first subpoint in that discussion.
> >
> > > i. Heading Three
> > >
> > > And more text that discusses the subpoint of that subpoint.

You can do this with the other approach as well, but the multilevel list option seems especially designed for this. And if you're using one of Word's pre-defined lists, it works fairly well. Spacing and formatting is consistent across the various levels.

What I do when I'm using one of these lists is I set up the number of levels I need (for example, above I have three levels) and then I use the Format Painter to assign the correct level to the other headers in my document. You can also use the multilevel list dropdown, just be sure you click on the list under Lists In Current Documents to be sure that you're actually using the same list throughout the whole document.

The tricky part to using these lists comes when you decide you want to use your own multilevel list with either custom numbering or custom formatting. I had a client who had a very, very specific list they wanted to use but had no documents set up with it, so users were constantly trying to recreate it in each new report they wrote and it took hours to get it right. The only way I ever found to make those reports work consistently was to start with a brand-new document where I'd created the multilevel list to their specifications and then copying in the text for each section, being careful to strip out any numbering or list in each copied section. Trying to build a custom multilevel list in a document that has already used a numbered list just doesn't work well.

If you ever do need to build a custom multilevel list, the option is there under the multilevel list dropdown.

Click on Define New Multilevel List and it will bring up the Define New Multilevel List dialogue box.

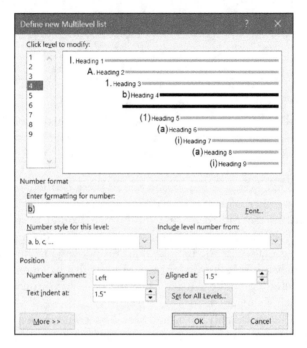

Defining each level of your list is pretty straightforward. Click on each level, choose the numbering style you want to use for that level, and then set your indents. Word will show you a preview of how all the levels you've set look. The problem is getting the lists to be stable within a Word document and to not have them revert to an unwanted format. All I can say is be sure to use any custom list you build in a new document and to only use that list. Don't try to combine different numbered lists in the same document when you're working with a custom multi-level list.

CONCLUSION

So that's the basics of lists in Word.
   If you get stuck, reach out at:

mlhumphreywriter@gmail.com

I'm happy to help. I don't check that email account every single day but I do check it regularly and will try to find you the answer if I don't know it.
   Good luck with it!

APPENDIX A: BASIC TERMINOLOGY

TAB

I refer to the menu choices at the top of the screen (File, Home, Insert, Design, Page Layout, References, Mailings, Review, View, Developer) as tabs. If you click on one you'll see that the way it's highlighted sort of looks like an old-time filing system.

CLICK

If I tell you to click on something, that means to use your mouse (or trackpad) to move the arrow on the screen over to a specific location and left-click or right-click on the option. (See the next definition for the difference between left-click and right-click).

If you left-click, this selects the item. If you right-click, this generally creates a dropdown list of options to choose from. If I don't tell you which to do, left- or right-click, then left-click.

LEFT-CLICK/RIGHT-CLICK

If you look at your mouse or your trackpad, you generally have two flat buttons to press. One is on the left side, one is on the right. If I say left-click that means to press down on the button on the left. If I say right-click that means press down on the button on the right.

Now, as I sadly learned when I had to upgrade computers and ended up with an HP Envy, not all track pads have the left- and right-hand buttons. In that case, you'll basically want to press on either the bottom left-hand side of the track pad or the bottom right-hand side of the trackpad. Since you're working blind it may take a little trial and error to get the option you want working. (Or is that just me?)

SELECT OR HIGHLIGHT

If I tell you to select text, that means to left-click at the end of the text you want to select, hold that left-click, and move your cursor to the other end of the text you want to select.

Another option is to use the Shift key. Go to one end of the text you want to select. Hold down the shift key and use the arrow keys to move to the other end of the text you want to select. If you arrow up or down, that will select an entire row at a time.

With both methods, which side of the text you start on doesn't matter. You can start at the end and go to the beginning or start at the beginning and go to the end. Just start at one end or the other of the text you want to select.

The text you've selected will then be highlighted in gray.

If you need to select text that isn't touching you can do this by selecting your first section of text and then holding down the Ctrl key and selecting your second section of text using your mouse. (You can't arrow to the second section of text or you'll lose your already selected text.)

DROPDOWN MENU

If you right-click in a Word document, you will see what I'm going to refer to as a dropdown menu. (Sometimes it will actually drop upward if you're towards the bottom of the document.)

A dropdown menu provides you a list of choices to select from.

There are also dropdown menus available for some of the options listed under the tabs at the top of the screen. For example, if you go to the Home tab, you'll see small arrows below or next to some of the options, like the numbered list option in the paragraph section. If you click on those arrows, you'll see that there are multiple choices you can choose from listed on a dropdown menu.

DIALOGUE BOX

Dialogue boxes are pop-up boxes that cover specialized settings. As just mentioned, if you click on an expansion arrow, it will often open a dialogue box that contains more choices than are visible in that section. When you right-click in a Word document and choose Font, Paragraph, or Hyperlink that also opens dialogue boxes.

Dialogue boxes allow the most granular level of control over an option. For example, the Paragraph Dialogue Box has more options available than in the Paragraph section of the Home tab.

(This may not apply to you, but be aware that if you have more than one Word document open and open a dialogue box in one of those documents, you may not be able to move to the other documents you have open until you close the dialogue box.)

CONTROL SHORTCUTS

I'll occasionally mention control shortcuts that you can use to perform tasks. When I reference them I'll do so by writing it as Ctrl + a capital letter. To use the shortcut just hold down the control key while typing the letter specified. Even though the letter will be capitalized, you don't need to use the capitalized version for the shortcut to work. For example, holding down the Ctrl key and the s key at the same time will save your document. I'll write this as Ctrl + S.

ABOUT THE AUTHOR

M.L. Humphrey is a former stockbroker with a degree in Economics from Stanford and an MBA from Wharton who has spent close to twenty years as a regulator and consultant in the financial services industry.

You can reach M.L. at mlhumphreywriter@gmail.com or at mlhumphrey.com.